J. M. YOUNG ARTS AND CRAFTS FURNITURE

181 Photographs

J. M. YOUNG FURNITURE COMPANY

EDITED BY
MICHAEL E. CLARK & JILL THOMAS-CLARK

D1606627

DOVER PUBLICATIONS, INC.

NEW YORK

Published in Canada by General Publishing Company, Ltd., 30 Lesmill Road, Don Mills, Toronto, Ontario.
Published in the United Kingdom by Constable and Company, Ltd., 3 The Lanchesters, 162–164 Fulham Palace Road, London W6 9ER.

Bibliographical Note

J. M. Young Arts and Crafts Furniture: 181 Photographs is a new work, first published by Dover Publications, Inc., in 1994.

Library of Congress Cataloging-in-Publication Data

J.M. Young arts and crafts furniture : 181 photographs / J.M. Young Furniture Company ; edited by Michael E. Clark and Jill Thomas-Clark.
    p. cm.
    1. J.M. Young Furniture Company. 2. Arts and crafts movement—New York (State) 3. Furniture—New York (State)—History—20th century. I. Clark, Michael E. II. Thomas-Clark, Jill. III. J.M. Young Furniture Company.
NK2439.J14J14   1994
749.147'62—dc20   93-51499
ISBN 0-486-27840-9 (pbk.)   CIP

Manufactured in the United States of America
Dover Publications, Inc., 31 East 2nd Street, Mineola, N.Y. 11501

Photo and Collection Credits

DEDICATION

This work is dedicated to Neil Wright and Frances Wright, who had the foresight to preserve the records of the J. M. Young Furniture Company for posterity; to Gordon Young, whose recollections provided a special insight into the day-to-day operation of the J. M. Young Furniture Company; and to the memory of Dorothy Young, who had faith that this publication would be completed.

ACKNOWLEDGMENTS

It is impossible to put together any work such as this without the help of a large number of sources. Our first major source of information was Roy Snyder, Camden, New York's historian, who initially introduced us to the town and led us to important pieces of information. A significant contribution has come from Neil and Frances Wright, who preserved many of the company records. Loss of these records would have impoverished the history of the decorative arts in America. Gordon Young's recollections of his own work at the plant, starting as a young boy, have helped to clarify the period and added immeasurably to the interpretation and usefulness of the records. Other important records were kept by Clarence Young's stepson, George Williams, and his spouse, Norma Williams, who have provided us with photographs and documentation on Clarence Young. We would like to thank Roy Snyder for providing access to his unpublished notes, and Mr. Snyder, Neil Wright and Gordon Young for granting personal interviews in 1991 and 1992.

Among other experts on J. M. Young furniture, the antique dealers and collectors have given freely of their time and knowledge. David Rudd, of Dalton's Antiques, and Michael Ward and George Fontanals, of Forthright Furniture, have been a major source of information about Young and comparisons with other furniture companies. Dealers Mark Whitt, Mike Watts, Dwayne Colp, Jaime Pearce, Mark Prucha, Dan and Carol Evans, Rod McLean and Jim Hugunin have brought Young furniture to our attention and helped us to distinguish between Young's work and that of others. Auction houses and auctioneers have often been helpful in locating pieces and allowing us to measure and photograph them. Among these sources, our special thanks to Richard Savoia, of Savoia's, and Jeremy Caddigan, of Caddigan's Auctioneers. We are also indebted to David Numsey Otto and Howard Mansfield for providing us with photographs of some of the rarer work of the J. M. Young Company from their own collections, and to Kimberly A. Kozlowski, of Syracuse YMCA, for information and photographs of J. M. Young furniture *in situ.*

We would like to recognize Michael Danial, Corporate Historian of the L. & J. G. Stickley Company, for his advice and comments. We are deeply indebted also to Alfred and Aminy Audi, owners of L. & J. G. Stickley, for giving us permission to use the photograph of the no. 572 checker table from their company's *Craftsman and Handcraft Designs Catalog,* 1922. This assistance is clearly in the tradition of past cooperation between the L. & J. G. Stickley and J. M. Young and Sons companies.

A special note of thanks also goes to Bruce Johnson, coordinator of the annual Arts and Crafts Conference at the Grove Park Inn in Asheville, North Carolina, who has provided us with invaluable advice and support on this project, and to Nicholas Williams and Jan Kather for their photography of the pieces not appearing in the retail plates. Finally, our deep indebtedness to Elmira College, Elmira, New York, for providing the special funding and sabbatical leave to complete this project. The history of the decorative arts movement in America owes this institution a special footnote of gratitude.

DR. MICHAEL E. CLARK AND JILL THOMAS-CLARK

CONTENTS

PREFACE: PRIMARY SOURCE MATERIAL

In 1991, we were fortunate to come across a cache of the records of the J. M. Young Furniture Company. The early company daily sales journals are complete from May 1896 to March 1930 except for the critical period from June 1900 to September 1904. Journals are missing from early 1930 through 1936, but complete from 1936 through 1972. The major surviving correspondence is from 1922 through 1929, when L. & J. G. Stickley and W. L. Babcock were forming their relationship with the J. M. Young Company, and from 1938 to 1939. In addition, other bits and pieces of earlier and later correspondence have survived.

A large number of preserved retail plates show the company's work throughout its history. Although some plates are missing, many objects with style numbers may not have had retail plates. While we have included a few transitional pieces, such as mission works with turned legs, many of the plates fall outside of our focus on J. M. Young's mission line. We also found two small books containing measurements and design changes handwritten by J. M. and George Young. Notes about stain formulas and finishes appeared in the sales journals.

We have collected a major part of the material on the J. M. Young Furniture Company, yet feel that there is undoubtedly more material to be uncovered and preserved for future scholars. We welcome and appreciate further information, pictures of pieces, and so on, and encourage individuals to contact us about their discoveries.

Introduction

Amid the diversity of the Arts and Crafts movement two major tenets remained constant: simplicity of form and quality of craftsmanship. Although a number of artists achieved these objectives, Gustav Stickley mastered them. As a result, his work was widely imitated during its own period. Gustav's younger brother, Leopold, in fact set up his own plant in Fayetteville, New York, where he recreated the work of his brother to finish out the remainder of Gustav's contract with the Tobey Furniture Company, Chicago.[1] His other brother, John George, joined Leopold in 1904 to form the L. & J. G. Stickley Co., Inc. Working under the trademark "Onondaga Shops," their line remained imitative and derivative: "But regardless of design, the furniture of the Onondaga Shops is always extremely well made, utilizing the finest-grained quarter-sawn and fumed-finished white oak, and compares quite favorably in this respect with Gustav's early pieces."[2] A product of Gustav Stickley's "enormous legacy," "[t]he contribution of the firm of L. & J. G. Stickley to the evolution and popularization of the design aesthetic of the American Arts and Crafts movement has long been underestimated."[3]

Other companies in the Syracuse area produced pieces that were imitative and derivative of the work of both Gustav Stickley and L. & J. G. Stickley. Some of these companies failed miserably to match the Stickleys' simplicity and quality, but others came very close. One such firm was the J. M. Young Furniture Company of Camden, New York. The work of this small business and its contribution to the longevity of the Arts and Crafts movement have been long overlooked. Although its mission line was mostly derivative and imitative of the Stickleys, its individualized nonproduction pieces often came closer to the spirit of the handcrafted ideals of John Ruskin and William Morris.

Because of its craftsmanship and strong Stickley influence, the furniture of J. M. Young has caught the eye of many collectors. For example, Bruce Johnson noted that Young's no. 186 morris chair could be offered as an "affordable" alternative to the no. 332 Gustav Stickley original: "[Its] proportions aren't quite as pleasing, but remove the castors, have it upholstered in leather and you have an Arts & Crafts Morris chair to be proud of."[4] The following year, Johnson praised two J. M. Young no. 381 side chairs, and felt that the "firm . . . deserves additional research and recognition, as these chairs demonstrate."[5] The no. 381 side chair, a derivation of the L. & J. G. Stickley no. 808 side chair, was seen as an equally good alternative.

Our research has shown that the Youngs, beyond just designing pieces similar to the work of the Stickleys during the Arts and Crafts period, produced furniture based on and copied from particular Stickley pieces after 1922, when L. & J. G. Stickley ceased production of its mission line. This imitation began and continued with the full knowl-

1. L. & J. G. Stickley, *Early L. & J. G. Stickley Furniture,* 1992: Introduction by Donald A. Davidoff, ix.
2. *op. cit.:* x.
3. *op. cit.:* vii.
4. Bruce Johnson, *Grove Park Inn Arts and Crafts Conference Catalog,* 1990: 20.
5. Johnson, *Conference Catalog,* 1991: 41.

edge and encouragement of the Stickley company and its representatives, continuing the tradition of the Stickley mission line well into the twentieth century.

Beyond the quality, craftsmanship and similarity of its pieces to the work of the Stickleys, the importance of the J. M. Young Furniture Company lies in its unique production history: Young consistently produced a line of mission furniture longer than any other known commercial firm in the United States: from October 1904 (perhaps earlier) through the 1940s. Its enormous productivity over this period helps to account for the frequent appearance of Young pieces in the current marketplace.

A HISTORY OF THE J. M. YOUNG COMPANY

The J. M. Young Furniture Company was founded by John McIntosh Young (Fig. 1), a Scottish immigrant who settled north of Syracuse, in Camden, New York, in 1865, at the age of twenty. Soon after arriving, he settled into a job with the local F. H. Conant and Son Furniture Company as a woodcarver for the elaborate Victorian work of the period. According to John's grandson, Gordon Young, John learned his woodcarving skills in Scotland. However, John made a pact with his new employer to work on the condition that he also be given a variety of jobs in the plant "to learn the business."

Fig. 1: John M. Young (1845–1926)

By 1868, John had married Nancy Baldwin, with whom he was to have four sons: Aaron, Clarence, George and Vincent. In March 1872, John left the Conant Company and set up his own factory outside of Camden. Although the factory burned down in 1878, John Young soon formed a partnership with J. M. Dexter and moved the company into the town of Camden. On Dexter's retirement in 1888, the company became known as the J. M. Young Furniture Company.

By that year, the company's speciality was "center tables of which there are more than a dozen styles including wood and marble top. . . . Mr. Young makes all classes of cabinet work, such as book-cases, side-boards, and bedroom sets."[6] The retail plates for various center tables and chairs have survived. Most of the tables are elaborately carved. The chairs range from the normal pressed-back late-Victorian sidè chairs and fancy rockers to the standard claw-footed morris chair.

At least one of these early chair designs seems to tie it to the Aesthetic movement, indicating that John was aware of alternative design styles. One document, a receipt for lodging and meals, in fact places John Young in London for a week in August 1899. With no known relatives there, and no clues to the reason for the trip, we can only speculate on Young's encounters and activities—as we do for Gustav Stickley's similarly unexplained

6. *Camden Advance-Journal,* 1888.

London visit the year before.[7] Certainly, both furniture makers would have become aware of advances in the Aesthetic and the Arts and Crafts movements in the decorative arts in England. (Moreover, Gordon Young has indicated that his grandfather made several trips back to Scotland, often waiting in London for his ship to take him back.) With his periodic visits to New York City's annual furniture exposition[8] and his proximity to Gustav Stickley's activities in Syracuse, we can reasonably assume that John Young was familiar with the newest advances of his business and the essence of Stickley's Arts and Crafts philosophy.

One J. M. Young chair, found in the factory attic, illustrates this assumption. It is from this early period and bears a beautifully hand-carved floral back rail. Although such individuality in the creation of pieces is generally rare within most companies, this was not true for the small J. M. Young Company, which frequently turned out pieces to order in various sizes and designs. From the company's books and correspondence, it is clear that much of the case work was done on special order. Production pieces were often enlarged or cut to size for a customer; in other cases, a customer's rough drawing formed the basis of a custom design. Gordon Young mentions frequent trips with his uncle George Young to Masonic lodges to measure rooms so that the furniture could be made to fit its environment. An individualized twenty-foot-plus no. 272 drop-arm settle was not unusual. It was just such individuality in the creation of pieces on a retail basis that separated this company from its competitors.

During the years between 1890 and 1902, the company began to prosper selling its Victorian line. In 1890, George Young joined the firm (Fig. 2). To accommodate the growth, a new factory building was built, with the new name of John M. Young and Son printed on its side (Fig. 3). In 1901, a building to house stock lumber was constructed just east of the factory, and a large

Fig. 2: George W. Young (1869–1951)

Fig. 3: J. M. Young and Son factory, Camden, N.Y., ca. 1909

storehouse was moved to a location north of the factory.[9] A periodical souvenir of Camden describes the factory as "comparatively new and fully equipped with necessary machinery driven by steam power [which] was planned by Mr. J. M. Young. It is a substantial, well constructed building better arranged for the comfort of the workmen especially in the matter of light and air space,

7. Mary Ann Smith, Gustav Stickley: The Craftsman, 1983: 9.

8. Camden Advance-Journal, 11 July 1901.
9. Camden Advance-Journal, 18 July 1901.

than is common in factories where a great amount of machinery is required."[10]

In 1902, Clarence Young joined the company as bookkeeper (Fig. 4). The company became known as J. M. Young and Sons, and its early labels—white, with serrated edges—indicated the name change. A year later,

Fig. 4: Clarence E. Young (1880–1958)

the industry noted that the Youngs had installed a tenon machine.[11] The Youngs continued to be both innovative and concerned for their workers at the same time. According to Neil Wright, an elaborate ventilation system was installed to keep dust to a minimum. Roy Snyder wrote that, when electric power came to Camden in 1920, "the J. M. Young chair factory was the first mill in town to completely power its machinery with electricity."[12] Gordon Young indicated that the company had its own drying kilns, fuming chambers, steamers for bending wood and much of the equipment necessary to complete a product from start to finish. For a small company that generally employed no more than 12 to 14 workers, it was clearly modern for its size by early twentieth-century standards. However, in spite of all

the machinery, Gordon had still maintained that most of the work was hand-fitted and finished.

The Youngs maintained a close relationship between the workers and their products, even encouraging design suggestions made by the workers. Between workers and management, we are left with the distinct impression that relationships were friendly and congenial. One must keep in mind that the Youngs, unlike the Stickleys, worked in the factory for all of their professional lives; theirs was a true family-run, family-operated business. Family involvement was true of the workers as well, for payroll records verify the employment of several members of a single family: brother and brother, father and son, husband and wife.

These close ties carried over into the relationship between J. M. Young and other furniture companies. Both the Conant Furniture Company and the Harden Chair Company bought wood, leather, nails, horsehair, stain and dowels from J. M. Young on a regular basis. Gordon Young mentions that the Harden Chair Company, which had set up an operation in Camden to manufacture its mission line, often made some of their mortise-and-tenon joints on Young equipment. He recalls that Charley Harden came over to the factory and made many of the joints himself. Perhaps it is for this reason that some construction problems and techniques are common to the two companies. For example, it seems that neither company owned a machine to create dovetail joints for drawers. As a result, each company had to solve the problem in its own way. This cooperation between companies foreshadowed the eventual close relationship between the Youngs and L. & J. G. Stickley.

The Young factory was located on a side track that allowed the firm direct access to the rest of the Northeast by train: "They are manufacturing tables and chairs to an extent which gives them a trade direct with retailers over a section of country covering a considerable portion of New York, Pennsylvania and the New England states."[13] Surveys of

10. *"Grips" Historical Souvenir of Camden, N.Y.,* 1902: 104.
11. "Eastern Notes," *Furniture World,* 12 November 1903.
12. Roy Snyder, *Camden Chronology,* 1984: 186.
13. "Grips,": 104.

the company journals and ledgers confirm that the sales area before and during the period from 1904 to 1926 was chiefly the northeastern portion of the country. The impressive New England sales were largely the result of Young's aggressive sales representatives, J. C. and G. F. Weatherly, who virtually built up Young's mission line in that area. It was these men who were responsible for picking up major contracts with firms like Jordan Marsh in Boston and G. Fox in Hartford, Connecticut.

At the turn of the century, Gustav Stickley made radical changes in furniture design and form, producing this new line of furniture in Eastwood, New York, just south of Camden. The Youngs followed directly in his footsteps. At some point before October 1904, they began to produce the first of their own mission line of furniture. The existing daily journals for this period, begun in October 1904, list the style number of each object, its current price, location sold, finish and fabric. The initial 1904 journal lists a number of objects that are clearly Arts and Crafts in design and are derivative in design and construction of the work of Gustav Stickley.

Although the first Arts and Crafts object that can be securely correlated between the retail photographic plates and the 1904 daily journals is the no. 150 rocker, the most significant is J. M. Young's no. 186 morris chair (Fig. 5). (This version does not appear in the retail plates.) It is clearly derivative of

Fig. 5: Young's no. 186, 5-slat morris chair, early version

Gustav Stickley's no. 332 reclining chair, which appeared in 1902. While many companies produced their own version of this morris chair (the L. & J. G. five-slat version was the no. 498 reclining chair), what is particularly interesting about Young's no. 186 is not only how close it came to the Gustav original in size and construction initially but how popular the chair remained and how it evolved over the duration of the Arts and Crafts period. In one form or another, no. 186 remained in the J. M. Young Arts and Crafts line from 1904 through the 1940s. The ledgers indicate that it was also sold as a frame "in the white" to be completed by the customer. The daily journals indicate that between 1904 and 1913 at least 1,350 chairs and frames of this model were sold.

The proportions and measurements of no. 186's early version are similar, but not identical, to the Gustav original, overall measuring one inch smaller. For example, for the height of the back from the floor, the Gustav measures 40″; no. 186, 39″. For the height of the seat from the floor, the Gustav measures 16″; no. 186, 15″. The Gustav's seat size is 23″w × 27″d; no. 186: 22″w × 26″d. (Later versions had different measurements.)

The earliest models of no. 186 have five slats on the side, like the Gustav original. The design of the distinctive sharp cuts to back of the flat arms and pegged supports are the same in both models, as are the laminated posts, which show the full effect of the quarter-sawn oak. No. 186 uses hinged supports on the bottom of the back rather than the pegged arrangement. Corbels are used on the front and back posts of both models. Early no. 186 corbels measure 4 ⅞″ in length and a full 2″ in width at the top. These early corbels appear fat since they were cut from full one-inch stock and were pinned to the post with the traditional ⁵⁄₁₆″ dowels. The through-tenons on the arms of the early models are also large, measuring a full 2¾″ square. The seats in this early version were loose cushions of laced leather. The bottom cushion on the early versions was supported by springs wired to a frame and covered with canvas.

One disturbing feature of no. 186 is its false through-tenons on the rails. Although the joints are pegged mortise-and-tenon joints, the Youngs routed out holes with precision, then filled them with oak plugs to simulate through-tenons. (Both the Harden Company and the Quaint Art Company of Syracuse used this technique as well.) Although it seems it would have been easier to fit the tenon through the leg, Young's technique was used for production purposes. The company's design books indicate that the front rails of many chairs in production were the same size, making it more cost-effective to produce and stock-pile a single-size rail that would fit all chairs. Although the technique of routing out the material was time-consuming, it was still more efficient and appropriate than the cheaper appliqué method used by other companies. The end result of the design of the early five-slat no. 186 is a product that is very close to the Gustav original, suggesting Young's respect for Gustav's work. One could also make a similar case that Young's no. 182 trestle table, or the chairs from this period, owed much to Gustav's work.

Between 1905 and 1908, when Young's no. 200 series was introduced, a number of important design changes took place toward the end of the period that softened the company's line. It was a period of both imitation and experimentation, when changes were taking place throughout the various mission furniture lines in many companies. Young's no. 186 reflected some of those design changes. The seats were changed to the drop-in auto-spring seats that were also being utilized by L. & J. G. Stickley. The arms were softened by beveling. The through-tenons on the arm posts were reduced but remained pegged through the arms, as were all the rail joints. The peg arrangement that supported the back was changed to a bar that fit neatly into notched holes, as on the early Onondaga Shop morris chairs. The chairs now had four slats instead of the original five. The cushions no longer appeared with the lacing, but in smoothly edged Spanish leather of varying grades. The chairs also began to appear with fumed-oak finishes. The post corbels were lengthened to 8⅛" and were nailed, instead of pegged, to the leg posts. However, the laminated posts remained the same size, as did most other measurements. Some models have surfaced that have the front apron arched (Fig. 6); other later models have the ends of their arms rounded. The total effect is of a chair whose details resemble the later softening effects in the work of Harvey Ellis on the Craftsman line.

Fig. 6: Young's no. 186, 4-slat morris chair

This was also the period when Gustav Stickley was developing his "spindle" line of furniture. Interestingly enough, when asked to define the difference between Young's furniture and Stickley's, Gordon Young replied that Stickley's furniture often had thin slats and misproportioned pegs (e.g., dowels that held the joints together). Later, he specifically identified the thin slats as spindles. He noted that the spindle furniture was something that the Youngs "just didn't do." Whatever the reason, it was clearly a design preference to avoid spindles in favor of larger slats. In addition, the smaller ⁵⁄₁₆" dowels were preferred to Stickley's larger size. The firm did not adopt any lines that worked in the "prairie style" of Frank Lloyd Wright or L. & J. G.'s adaptations in that direction. Notwithstanding Young's resistance to these newer directions, this period did produce some experimentation: the no. 268 settle, with its inverted "V" shaped arms; the no. 288 rocker and no. 289 arm-chair, with its curved back; and the unusual no. 290 table.

As with most firms, design for the Youngs often seemed to correlate with marketability. But this practice for the Youngs, according to Gordon Young, meant that new designs and design modifications were often suggested by the salesmen. We have several notes from J. C. Weatherly suggesting changes in styles quite early in the mission period. (One series of letters from the 1920s complains that certain changes, as usual, had *not* been made after his pleasant visit to Camden!) Gordon also mentioned that workmen within the plant often suggested design changes as well. It does not appear that the Youngs often utilized the services of designers. The designing that did occur was more often through impromptu demonstrations by John Young and George Young in the factory. They worked much in the manner of Gustav Stickley, waving their hands to indicate size and proportion to others.

Although the Young designs did not include the spindled "prairie school" look, they did adapt to the softer arches. Gentle arches were added to the front seat rails of many chairs. The theme is also carried out in the grace of the no. 288 rocker and no. 289 ladder-back armchair, with their reversed-arch back top rail. With its gently arched top rails, the no. 206 footrest—an immediate success following its development in 1905—became a catalog staple. The ledgers indicate that the company sold 3,107 pieces between 1905 and 1919. The model did not go out of production, and appears on a 1925 price list. Interestingly enough, it bears a close resemblance to the L. & J. G. Stickley no. 396, varying only slightly in measurements.

Other pieces in the no. 200 series—specifically, the no. 284 open-arm morris chair and the no. 274 even-arm settle—indicate a close design connection with the work of L. & J. G. Stickley. Both of these pieces have a direct counterpart in the Onondaga Shops retail plates and the later L. & J. G. catalog.

The no. 284 is very similar in design to the Onondaga Shops no. 770 retail plate and to the no. 470 reclining chair that appears in the 1910 L. & J. G. catalog. In comparison with the no. 470, the major differences appear to be Young's longer corbels and the rounded arms. Also, the no. 284 is approximately one inch smaller in all measurements and has hinged supports on the back instead of the traditional peg supports used by L. & J. G; otherwise they appear to be the same. Both have auto-spring cushions, mortise-and-tenon joints with pegs, and generally are made of quarter-sawn fumed oak (although mahogany and other woods could be used on the no. 284 and on the no. 470 as well).

No. 284 quickly became a staple of the line with over a thousand pieces sold between its introduction in 1908 and 1919. It continued to be sold into the 1940s. This model served as a basis for a number of other chairs, including morris rockers listed under the same style number, the no. 285 open-arm stationary-back rocker, the no. 471 slatted morris chair, and the no. 475 slatted, stationary-back rocker. All have similarities to L. & J. G. counterparts. The no. 285 compares to the L. & J. G. no. 411. In the late 1920s, the firm introduced the no. 471 morris chair, which was based on the no. 284 frame but included five slats down the side.

Somewhat more mysterious is the connection between the no. 274 even-arm settle, its retail plate and a matching Stickley piece. The no. 274 appears to be identical to the L. & J. G. no. 281 settle, except that it is two inches longer. The retail plate for the no. 274 is a drawing that appears to be almost identical to the drawing in L. & J. G.'s 1910 catalog. The pillows in the J. M. Young drawing are different and there appear to be some shading differences. (This drawing is part of a series of drawings signed "Monroe 08." Monroe's name appears in the company's 1908 payroll records.)

Young's daily journals indicate that sales of the no. 274 began in 1908 and continued until 1929. Some of these models have surfaced in various antique shows. David Rudd, of Dalton's Antiques, has stated that they appear to be "less beefy" than the L. & J. G.

original. Although the early Young version used solid posts, later versions used the quadrilinear post construction of the L. & J. G. Stickley versions. In both cases, the posts were indeed smaller, as Rudd suggests. Although earlier versions appeared with solid or laminated posts, according to Rudd, all of the no. 230 even-arm settles and no. 272 drop-arm settles we have seen have quadrilinearly constructed posts, with labels dated after 1915. Michael Danial, the current L. & J. G. Corporate Historian, has noted that only J. M. Young and L. & J. G. Stickley used this type of post construction.

Young's construction was also very similar to that of the L. & J. G. line. In Syracuse, one of the tables drawn by Monroe has turned up with original L. & J. G. hardware. The tables had pegged joints, were made of quarter-sawn oak, and often had splined tops like their L. & J. G. counterparts. Thus, it is clear that many of the no. 200 series are derivative and could be confused with the work of L. & J. G. Stickley.

In the other series—nos. 300, 400 and even 500—we often find other similarities with the L. & J. G. line. For example, the no. 380 slipper rocker and the no. 381 chair (the one praised by Bruce Johnson) are frequently confused with the L. & J. G. no. 809 rocker and no. 808 chair. The simplicity of this design, with its softly rounded crest rail and arched side rails, is clearly similar to the Stickley version. Only when the chairs are placed next to each other do the similarities fade. This is particularly true of the rocker because the stretchers are offset on both models. But there are differences even beyond the telltale L. & J. G. curved corner blocks that support the spring-seat version. The front posts on the J. M. Young version are rectangular, while on the L. & J. G. version they are square. There are other differences, such as the height and width of stretchers. In the no. 400 series, one rocker (no. 456) and an armchair (no. 457) were frequently referred to in the journals as the "Stickley Chair" rather than by their style numbers. Again, both of these chairs are very similar to their L. & J. G. Stickley counterparts.

There were other, more personal, connections with the L. & J. G. Company. Gordon Young recalls that "Stickley" (Leopold, most likely?) visited the J. M. Young plant at least twice in 1913 or 1914, when Gordon was seven years old, discussing furniture with John and George Young for some time and in a very positive way. Gordon also recalls John's trips to the Stickley plant, occasions supported by various pieces of correspondence between the two companies in the 1920s. Given the obvious similarity in product design and the competition between the companies, one might expect these interactions to have been rather negative sessions. On the contrary, according to subsequent correspondence and evidence, the visits and conversations seem to have been friendly and the relationship positive between the Youngs and the Stickleys.

It was in the early 1920s that the relationship between the two companies became closer, with correspondence indicating that the Youngs were seeking the formula for the Stickley #2 fumed finish. Perhaps it was at this critical moment that Phillip Waldron appeared. Gordon Young remembers that Waldron, one of L. & J. G.'s finishers, quit the Stickley firm and came to work for the Youngs, bringing with him his knowledge of the Stickley finishes. (In the absence of clearer records, but given Gordon's youthful recollection of having worked with Waldron, we can only guess that he joined no later than the early 1920s. Young journals and ledgers do mention a "Stickley finish," but they also refer to a "Limbert finish.")

Times seemed to have been prosperous for the small company. Although the Youngs began to produce other styles in 1920, the mission line remained their best seller. The high quality of this furniture must have impressed L. & J. G. Stickley, as would the company's modernization when it converted to electricity in 1920, and added a 70-foot extension onto the mill in 1925.

John Young retired in 1924 and died in 1926. His two sons George and Clarence took over the company, which became known as John M. Young's Sons Furniture Company. The first surviving correspondence between J. M. Young and the L. & J. G. Stickley Company dates to a time just prior to John's death. On 21 November 1924, the Youngs wrote to L. & J. G. Stickley, asking about obtaining the contracts they had on mission furniture; L. & J. G. had stopped making the line in 1922. The Stickleys responded: "We have a considerable inventory on hand and so far have made no arrangements for turning over the contracts we have for mission furniture. However, should we do this, we will keep you before us and get in communication with you." The next letter, dated 7 February 1925, is from L. & J. G. Stickley. Evidently they had requested that J. M. Young build some furniture to sell under the Stickley name: ". . . we find that it will be impossible to have you build these pieces for the reason on the larger quantities your charge would be more than we get for these pieces, however we wish to thank you very kind [sic] for your attention in this matter and if any thing further comes up, we will be glad to give you a chance on these."

The Stickleys did give the Youngs additional business: a letter dated 26 January 1926 requests that "Mr. Young call on us tomorrow or Wednesday if possible regarding the making of some mission pieces for us." Subsequently there was a series of letters between the two companies, with J. M. Young asking advice on how to recreate some of their finishes and construction techniques, and on purchasing machinery and lumber. The letters are always cordial. For example, when there seemed to be some confusion on recreating the exact #2 Stickley fumed finish, the Stickleys told Young to drop by and they would sell him the stain and show him the method. Another letter from 1926 indicates that L. & J. G. Stickley sold the Youngs a seat-making machine on which they held the patent, and a shaper. It was with these machines that the Youngs were able to duplicate the Stickley wood seats and possibly aid in the construction of their quadrilinear posts for their settles. (However, the Youngs were using quadrilinear posts as early as 1915, at least ten years before the purchase of the shaper.) From

such letters it is clear that the Youngs were being encouraged to continue the Stickley tradition.

In March 1926, W. L. Babcock of New York City wrote to the J. M. Young's Sons Company on L. & J. G. Stickley stationery proposing that he become their representative in New York City. His letter states that he had been representing L. & J. G. in New York for "quite a number of years" selling their "fumed oak" line. A letter from the J. M. Young Company to Stickley requests their opinion, and a return letter from Stickley indicates that "Babcock has handled this end, for a number of years and has been entirely satisfactory to us." With this recommendation, Babcock became the J. M. Young representative. During the early part of the Youngs' business, their mission line had been built up in New England by the Weatherleys. Now it appears that Babcock would do the same for Young elsewhere.

Within a few months, Babcock was aggressively selling J. M. Young's furniture not only in New York but elsewhere, picking up business with General Electric, Western Union, A. T. & T., the F. W. Woolworth Company, the Anglo-Chilean Nitrate Company, John Wanamaker & Company, the Veterans Administration, the United States Navy and a number of other large organizations. Subsequently, Babcock's letterhead claimed to represent both Young and Stickley, referring to the Young's Sons Company as "makers of straight line oak and birch furniture" while the Stickleys were represented as "makers of Early American Furniture."

As L. & J. G. moved out of the manufacture of the mission line in the early twenties, the Youngs began to pick up their business through Babcock, often including the manufacture of items that either Gustav Stickley or L. & J. G. had produced. Letters to Young contained clippings from both the Gustav and L. & J. G. catalogs, requesting that a specific item be made, carrying Babcock's signature and usually including pictures from L. & J. G. Stickley's *Craftsman and Handcraft Design Catalog,* 1922. (According to Michael Danial, the company has a copy of this catalog.) For example, a series of letters between Babcock, J. M. Young's Sons and the L. & J. G. Stickley Company concerns the proper construction of the no. 572 checker table (Fig. 7). One of Babcock's letters includes a picture clipped out of the 1922 catalog. The correspondence from this period continues with requests from other firms directly to the Youngs for the Stickley pieces or Stickley-type furniture.

Fig. 7: Young's no. 572, checkerboard table

From the 1920s through the 1940s, with the consent of the Stickley firm, the Youngs continued to manufacture products that directly imitated the earlier Gustav and L. & J. G. pieces. One letter indicates that Stickley had sent the Youngs a rocker so that a copy could be made. Other letters mention Stickley catalogs and specific pieces, with page numbers and style numbers. There are also frequent references to Stickley patterns or about obtaining patterns. (For this reason, some J. M. Young style numbers correspond to numbers used in the Stickley catalogs.) Sometimes substitutions could be made for pieces already in production by the Young Company; in other cases, pieces were copied as faithfully as possible. One of Babcock's letters asks the Youngs to refer in the catalog to no. 599, the L. & J. G. Stickley "mouse-

hole" trestle table—"good sellers," according to Babcock. Soon the Young no. 599 trestle tables were in production and selling well. A survey of the retail plates will show numerous items that, like the no. 599, are similar to the Stickley line but were not produced until the 1920s. Although some Stickley items were in production very early, other items—such as the no. 471 morris chair, the no. 601 desk, the no. 558 taboret, the no. 524 table and the no. 295 daybed/couch—did not come out until the 1920s, carrying the same style numbers as the corresponding Stickley pieces.

Despite the firm's successful productivity, there do seem to have been limits as to what the J. M. Young Company could produce of the Stickley line. In Babcock's letter requesting a number of case pieces for export to the Anglo-Chilean Nitrate Company, he asks if they could furnish dressers, chiffoniers, buffets and servers: "They like Stickleys #735 and 736 Buffets." He goes on to note, "They will use a lot of your settles chairs and rockers. There is a question in my mind whether you are in a position to make case work. . . . They will use a table on the order of stickleys #599. . . ." The Youngs responded that they could not furnish the case work but would produce the other work, and the order for the other pieces went through. The Youngs could produce case work on a small basis, but they were limited when it came to mass production of such pieces. Some bookcases, like the L. & J. G. nos. 641 and 652, were made in limited numbers, and some case work was done for export to the Firestone rubber plantations in Liberia in 1927. The measurements for these bookcases and some sideboards appear in the Youngs' design books. However, these items were few in comparison to their chairs, settles, settees, magazine racks, tables, wastebaskets and costumers.

While the J. M. Young's Sons Furniture Company manufactured lines of furniture similar to that of other firms throughout the 1930s and 1940s, their mission line, as business or office furniture, remained a large part of their sales. Sales were made to various departments of the United States government and to firms all over this country and throughout the world. We have located government blueprints and specifications for mission morris chairs, rockers, armchairs and tables; Gordon has indicated that these specifications were often based on existing models. The Navy and Veterans Administration continued to be major customers from the 1920s through the 1940s and beyond. Even the American Embassy in Berlin had J. M. Young furniture. The Firestone plantations ordered fumed furniture because it held up better in the tropical climate. One can probably still find J. M. Young Arts and Crafts morris chairs and rockers in almost any place on the globe. In fact, company correspondence often reminds the purchaser that they *do* manufacture *other* types of modern furniture as well! A 1939 letter from the F. W. Woolworth Company suggested that Young might try dropping their mission line in favor of metal furniture. There is no record of the Youngs' response.

The company continued to manufacture its mission line, although the line was modified in both style and material. For example, it continued to manufacture much of the mission line in oak but also worked in birch and maple. Of course, during this time maple was quite popular and birch could be made to look like mahogany without mahogany's problems or expense. The mission oak line was finally discontinued after World War II. However, some mission style numbers continued to appear. For example, the no. 388 table, along with a number of the smaller chairs, seem to continue into the late 1950s.

George Young died in 1951, leaving his share of the partnership to Clarence's grandson, Gordon Young. Clarence passed away in 1958, leaving the firm in Gordon's hands. Gordon maintained control until 1973, when the plant was sold to Neil Wright. The firm continued to manufacture a line of furniture until 1979, when the plant closed and the buildings were razed to provide space for a parking lot and apartments.

In summary, the J. M. Young Furniture Company, in its hundred years of existence, carried the Arts and Crafts line of furniture through much of the twentieth century. The firm was a small family business that believed in quality and honesty in their products. The designs, proportions, woods and finishes were simple but well done, reflecting Arts and Crafts philosophy. Although it seems that neither John, George nor Clarence espoused the philosophy in the way that Gustav Stickley articulated it in his publications, the Youngs still produced a handcrafted product that Gustav Stickley would probably have liked as much as L. & J. G. Stickley did. This small family business has left a significant legacy in the decorative arts by extending the life of the Arts and Crafts movement well beyond its once presumed death in the 1920s.

IDENTIFYING J. M. YOUNG FURNITURE

LABELS

Over the course of its hundred-year history, the J. M. Young Company had seven known labels. Five of these labels usually appear on mission pieces. The first reported label is rectangular and reads "J. M. Young and Son, Camden, N.Y." Although the authors have never seen the label, David Rudd, of Dalton's Antiques, reported seeing it on some early mission pieces. The label would have dated from after 1890, when George Young joined the company, and would have continued until Clarence joined the company in 1902, when it became known as J. M. Young and Sons Furniture Company.

The first label with the new name designation is a small, white rectangle with serrated edges, measuring $1'' \times 2''$, with the words

"J. M. Young & Sons, Camden, N.Y." (Fig. 8a). This label also has a "No." designation to be filled in with the style number of each piece. In use at least until 1915 or 1916, it is the most common label on the earlier pieces.

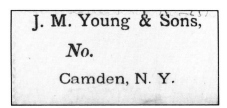

Fig. 8a: J. M. Young & Sons, white, serrated label
(*ca.* 1902–*ca.* 1916)

A second white label followed some time after 1915–16 (Fig. 8b). It measures 2″ × 3″, with the words "J. M. Young & Sons, Camden, N.Y.," and includes spaces for the style number, finish and cover designations. The type is larger than that of the first label and is framed by a black border.

Fig. 8b: J. M. Young & Sons, white, rectangular label
(*ca.* 1916–*ca.* 1920)

The third label is a black oval enscribed in florid gold script with a gold border (Fig. 8c). It measures 2″ × 3″, with the words "J. M. Young & Sons, Chair Manufacturers, Camden, New York." and includes printed boxes for finish, cover and style number. This style and design suggests that the label came into use at the end of the decade. It was used until J. M. Young retired in 1924 when the company became known as J. M. Young's Sons. The new letterhead was printed in a similar script.

Fig. 8c: J. M. Young & Sons, oval label
(*ca.* 1920–*ca.* 1926)

At this point, the company introduced a second black, oval label, reflecting its name change (Fig. 8d). Otherwise, it was identical in design to its predecessor. This label remained in use into the 1940s on mission furniture. Non-mission pieces from this period used an oval, white label. After the late 1930s, the proverbial "Do Not Remove" tags came into use and appeared on the bottom of all seats carrying the J. M. Young's Sons name.

Fig. 8d: J. M. Young's Sons, oval label (*ca.* 1926–1940s)

Labels were usually affixed to the front apron of very early chairs, on the back rail of later chairs, and on the bottom of hard or wood seats. They can also be found on the front edge of the aprons of small tables, on the underside of the bottom stretcher of tables, and on the underside of table tops and piano benches. On settles or settees, they may be found on the back or front rails or on the support beam between the rails. Labels were glued on and not tacked in place.

CONSTRUCTION

Construction techniques are also helpful in identifying J. M. Young furniture. The joints on all of the furniture that we have seen are mortise-and-tenon joints. These joints are either pegged with $5/16''$ birch dowels or pinned with steel pins. The way that joints are pegged varies from model to model. For example, all the rail joints are pegged on both the front and side rails of the no. 186 morris chair, while on the nos. 284 or 471 morris chair only the front rails are pegged. All post tenons through the arms are pegged from the side. The tops of these tenons and all posts usually have a distinctive pyramid shape, but some posts do have flat chamfered tops (such as on the no. 460 plant stand). Early chairs—such as the no. 100 series and early versions of the no. 200 series—have large post tenons and sharp edges on the arms. Later chairs have chamfering on the front arms and smaller post tenons. As a general rule, the later the piece the more the chamfering occurs.

The back rails of most chairs are usually steam-bent, with a few exceptions. Distinctly unlike most Stickley chairs, the bottom rails for most J. M. Young chairs and settees are not offset but form a square. However, this is not an absolute rule and there are some notable exceptions. For instance, the no. 380 rocker and no. 381 side chairs are often confused with corresponding Stickley versions, and the no. 456 rocker and no. 457 armchair—referred to as the "Stickley Chair" in Young's daily journals and design books—have offset stretchers.

Under their arms, most chairs have corbels that vary in length. Generally speaking, the corbels on the early pieces are short and fat. As the furniture designs evolved, the corbels became longer and thinner, reaching a length of $10\frac{1}{2}''$. Thus a chair can be found with short, medium or long corbels, depending on the date of its manufacture. The early corbels are pegged in the Gustav Stickley manner, but later models are pinned. Rails for the backs of morris chairs are not pegged. Most other chairs usually are pegged on the top rail. Again, one will find exceptions to this rule on various models.

Tenons are usually not full through-tenons, but are wooden plugs that fit into precisely routed-out holes. Wooden seats and table tops are usually attached with screws through the rails. Late wood seats are scalloped identically to the L. & J. G. Stickley wood seats (J. M. Young had purchased a patented seat-making machine from L. & J. G. around 1926). However, the seats are still screwed in from the rails rather than from the corner blocks, like L. & J. G.'s no. 960 chair. Corner blocks, trapezoidal in shape, are usually nailed and glued to the rails.

Drawers in tables rely on a rabbet joint rather than on dovetailing. Early versions of this joint are pegged while later versions are pinned. The Young company never owned a dovetail machine, and the cost of such handwork would have been prohibitive. This method of pegging drawers had been common since the turn of the nineteenth century, when such machinery was neither available nor affordable for small companies.

The bottom stretcher of tables like the nos. 210 and 388 is pegged from the underside of the bottom rail. Tops for tables may either be butt-jointed or splined in the L. & J. G. manner. For example, all no. 599 tables appear to be splined. Posts can be solid, laminated or of quadrilinear construction. Generally speaking, the posts for the no. 186 are laminated, and quadrilinear construction appears on models after 1915 of various settles such as the nos. 230, 272 and 274. However, the early models of these settles, like the early no. 186 morris chair, had solid or possibly laminated posts. Settees and chairs other than the early no. 186 had solid posts. Seats in many of the early chairs were made of loose cushions supported by a frame or simply tied and nailed to the rails. Later chairs utilized auto-spring drop-in seats.

WOODS

J. M. Young's furniture used a variety of woods. Generally speaking, the most common material found in their mission furniture is quarter-sawn oak, with plain-sawn oak used in places that were not generally visible—such as the side and back rails of chairs. However, some mission pieces were made of plain-sawn oak, walnut, cherry, birch and mahogany.

FINISHES

In the primary source material, we have found a number of formulas and references to stains, pointing to the wide variety of finishes used throughout the Young line. Period Arts and Crafts pieces seemed to use a fumed oak with a dark reddish stain, a dark Early English stain, weathered oak or a golden oak. The fumed oak and its variations were the most popular during the period. During the 1920s, the fumed oak stain was obtained directly from L. & J. G., and thus most pieces from that period will have an affinity for the L. & J. G. colors. This is especially so for the L. & J. G. #2 fumed oak stain, which was often requested by customers specifically. Work done during and after the late twenties often used birch stained to look like walnut, mahogany and maple.

A variety of varnishes and shellacs were used along with a coat of wax as a finish. Gordon Young mentions that for some pieces their furniture finishers ground out the soft part of the oak with wire brushes, then filled the spaces to provide for a high-gloss, smooth finish. All work was hand-rubbed. One particularity of Young's work was the lack of finishing on the bottoms of rails, stretchers and arms. A good way to identify a piece with an original finish is simply to flip it over and check to see if the underside of the rail has been stained. Generally speaking, many of the finishes have not worn well with time. In many cases, this may be due to the fact that the pieces were not done by J. M. Young but by others. Many pieces were shipped out of the plant "in the white" to be finished by the retailer or individual customers. With this in mind, one might find almost any finish on a piece of J. M. Young furniture.

About the Retail Plates

The following section contains 152 retail plates of mission furniture, a price list, a brochure, Veterans Administration blueprints and a concluding table of all known style numbers in J. M. Young's mission line (see p. 87).

The retail plates, which were found along with the primary source material about the J. M. Young Company, do not represent all pieces of the company's mission line. Many retail plates are missing or were never made. Some plates indicate the dimensions of a piece while others do not. In many cases, the sizes listed on the plates are inaccurate. This may be explained by the handcrafted nature of the object, or by the fact that a redesigned piece was not rephotographed. One must keep in mind that any artist's work has a tendency to evolve over a period of time, and that small changes in size may occur as the work evolves. (The previous discussion of the no. 186 morris chair and its evolution is a prime example.) Where a style number appears twice on one page—such as No. 186, page 24–the retail plates reflect variations that occurred over a period of time. Also, we should consider that model size was not listed on a retail plate until Babcock's request for that information, in 1926.

We have arranged the retail plates not by style number in sequential order but by type of object: individual chairs and rockers; matching chairs and rockers; morris chairs; parlor sets; miscellaneous settees, settles and daybeds; tables; umbrella stands, wastebaskets and plant stands; and footstools, bookcases and magazine racks. Although many style numbers do suggest a sequential creation, many do not. The best way to determine the date or size of an object is to refer to the table. Many objects with low style numbers were not produced until the 1920s, when the company took over the Stickley contracts, and some style numbers may have been changed to suit Babcock and make them correspond to the Stickley catalog numbers. Also, some objects—such as the no. 154 rocker and no. 155 armchair—are later reproductions of a similar model made by the F. S. Harden Company.

Thus, a word of caution on using the retail plates for identification. The collector should be aware that variations on the designs were frequently made to suit the customer and creator of the piece. For example, the no. 210 table may or may not have side slats, or the no. 436 footrests could have had stretchers and notched posts. One may also find a table or chair with or without through-tenons while its retail plate may show only one or the other of these details. Some pieces, such as the no. 381 side chair, could come with a wide variety of alterations. Some design orders call for arms, upholstered backs, solid-wood seats and flat top rails

rather than the crested norm. Style numbers could also indicate minor changes that do not appear in the plates. For example, the no. 370½ does not show through-tenons in the arms, but a no. 370 has surfaced with normal, complete pyramidal tenons.

In identifying the works through the retail plates and the table, one will find the diversity of the artist-craftman at work. J. M. Young, his sons and collective of craftsmen, working in the spirit of the Arts and Crafts movement, often made many design modifications on the spot to create an individualized piece. Although the company was a business and built production-line furniture as well as one-of-a-kind pieces, each object somehow had the individual touch of the artist himself. The end result, reflecting Gustav Stickley's philosophy, was, as Leopold Stickley might say of his own art, "simple furniture built along mission lines."

PIECES IN LIMITED PRODUCTION

In addition to the items shown in the government blueprints for the Veterans Administration (pp. 82–85), some additional pieces may have been one of a kind or few in number. For example, the no. 285 fixed-back morris rocker (Fig. 9) had a very limited

production. Only a handful have been found in the books with this style number, although a few more have been listed as no. 284 morris rockers with fixed backs. The two-over-four chest of drawers (Fig. 10) may be one of a kind, with real pegged through-tenons simi-

Fig. 9: Young's no. 285, fixed-back rocker

Fig. 10: Young, chest of drawers

lar to the Gustav Stickley no. 627 chest of drawers. The piano bench (Fig. 11)—listed only as "piano bench," without a style number—also had a limited production. (Interestingly, the piano bench has real, pegged, through-tenons and cross-bracing on the ends.)

Fig. 11: Young, piano bench

Researching the J. M. Young Company
Written Sources Cited in the Text

Camden Advance-Journal. Camden, New York: 1888; 11 July 1901; 18 July 1901.
"Eastern Notes" in *Furniture World.* New York: 12 November 1903.
"Grips" Historical Souvenir of Camden, N. Y. Camden, New York: 1902.
Johnson, Bruce. "Affordable Arts and Crafts" in *Grove Park Inn Arts and Crafts Conference Catalog.* Durham, North Carolina: Knock on Wood Publications, 1990.
————"The Grove Park Inn Collection: A Walking Tour" in *Grove Park Inn Arts and Crafts Conference Catalog.* Asheville, North Carolina: Bruce Johnson, 1991.
Smith, Mary Ann. *Gustav Stickley: The Craftsman.* New York: Dover Publications, Inc., 1992.
Snyder, Roy A. *Camden Chronology.* Camden, New York: 1984.
Stickley, L. & J. G. *Craftsman and Handcraft Designs Catalog.* Syracuse, New York: 1922.
————*Early L. & J. G. Stickley Furniture: From Onondaga Shops to Handcraft.* Davidoff, Donald A., and Robert L. Zarrow, eds. New York: Dover Publications, Inc., 1992.
The Young Family. Unpublished daily sales journals for J. M. Young and Sons Furniture Company and for J. M. Young's Sons Furniture company: 1904–1930; 1937–1972.

THE RETAIL PLATES

188

189

380

381

640

641

913

913½

1340

485

627

500

150

152

154

155

158½

160½

288

289

364

366

368½

370½

386

386½

425

424

424ws

448

449

454

455

456

457

1916

1917

1919

957

660

663

358

412

422

384

572

590

628

186

186

264

264

265

284

284

352

429

428

471

475

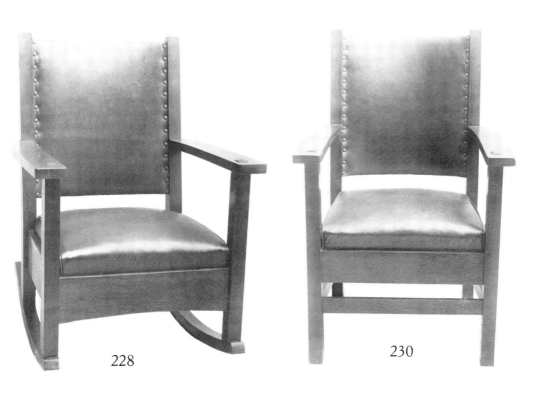

228

230

416

308

310

334

336

338

372

378

379

426

418

419

420

430

431

433

436

437

435

445

446

447

467

466

468

482

483

484

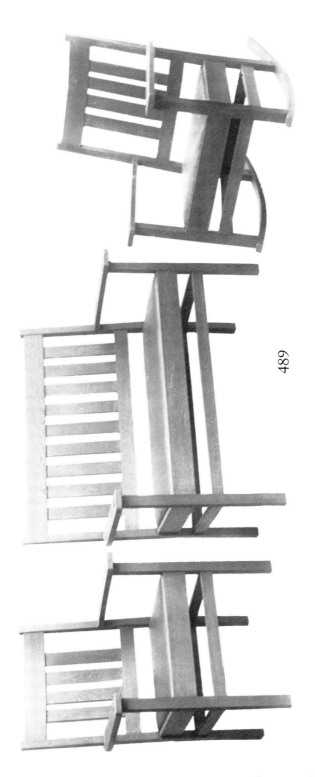

489

492

493

494

501

500

502

518

519

520

566

567

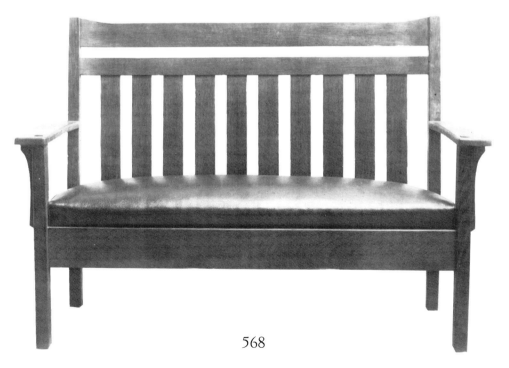

568

582

583

584

184

402

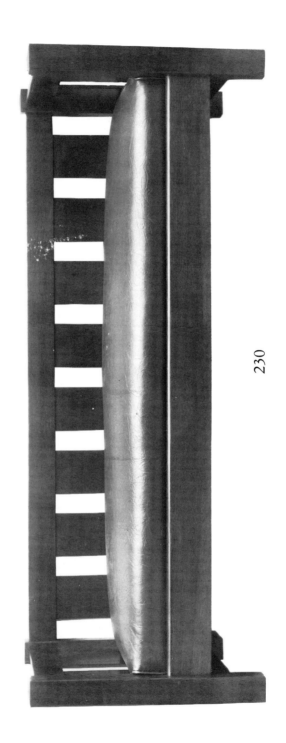

230

48

Settles

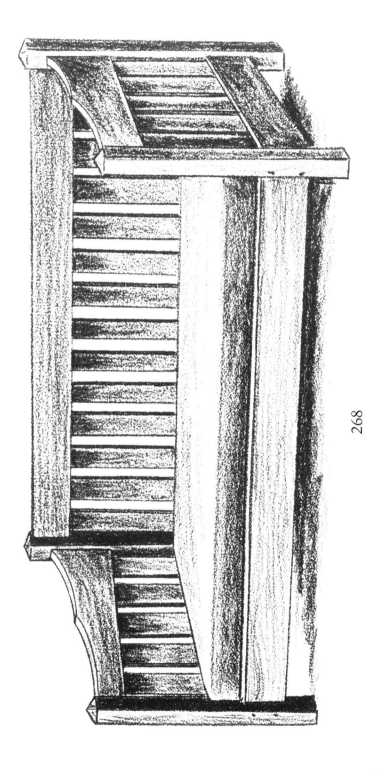

268

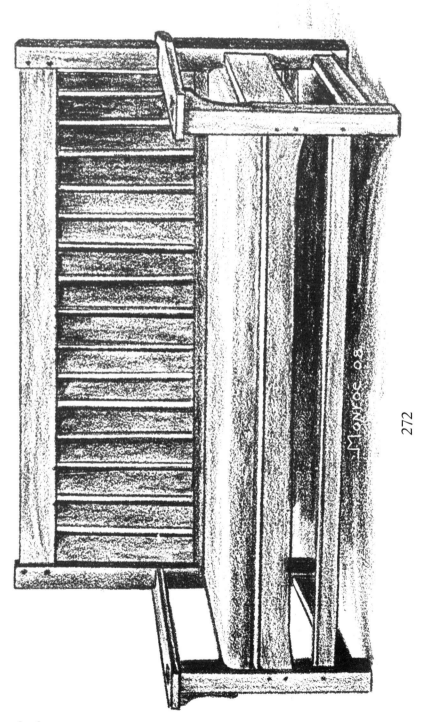

272

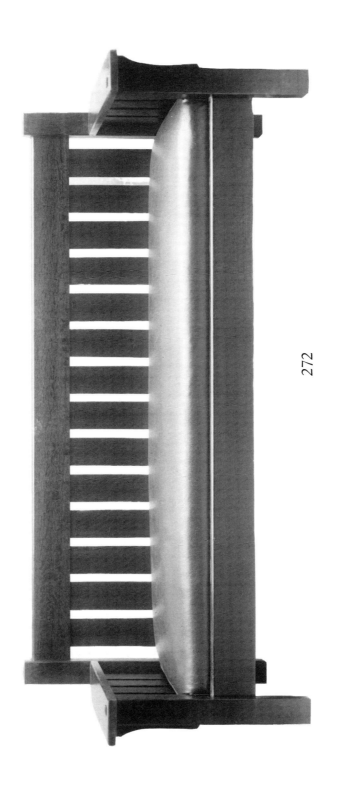

272

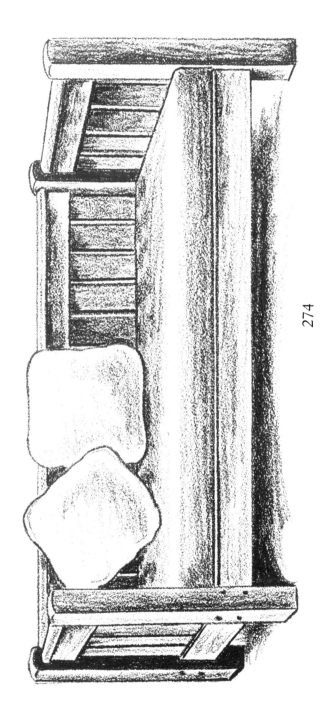

274

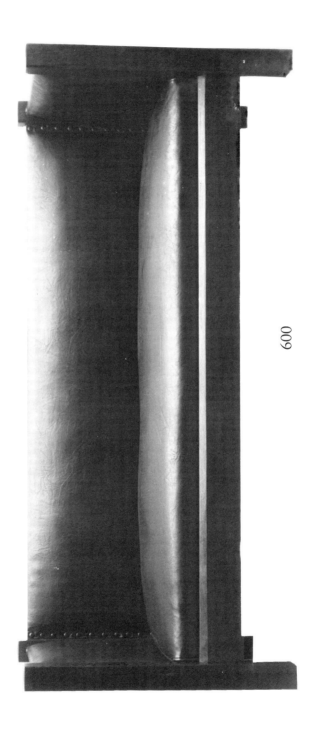

600

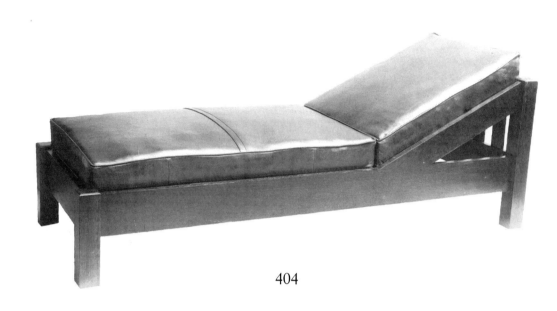

404

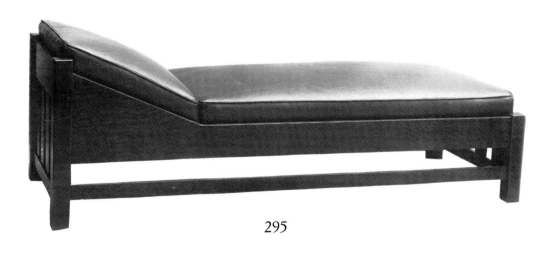

295

558

342

180

276

278

182

599

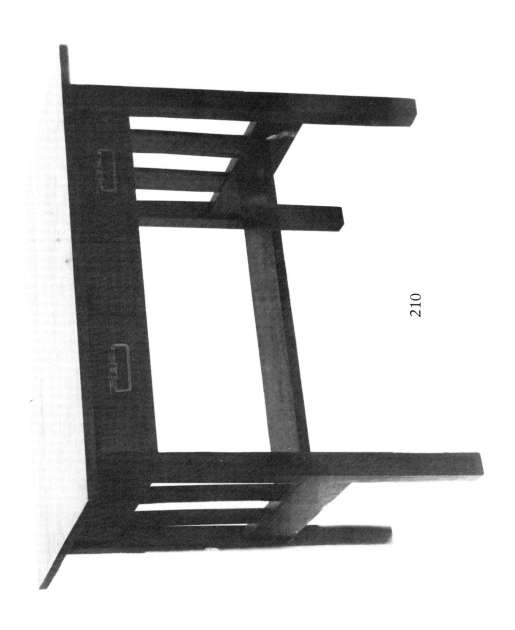

210

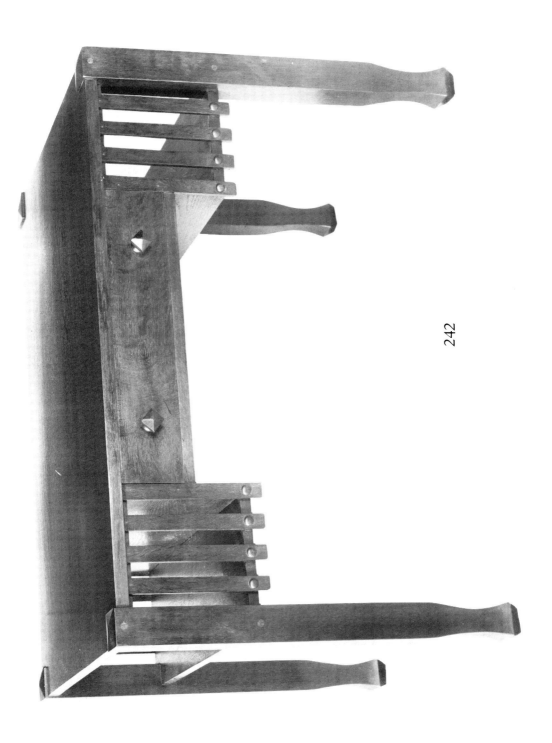

242

290

208

434

374

389

390

388

392

480

Table 65

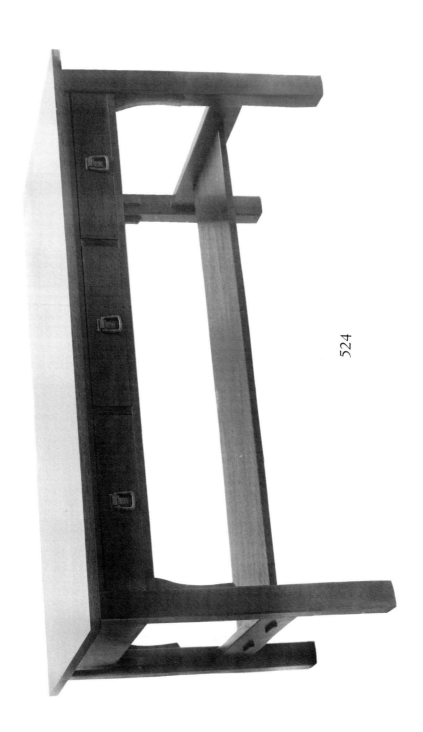

524

601

661

103

664

382

206

397

436

240

452

452

Sectional Bookcase [no number]

2

3

204

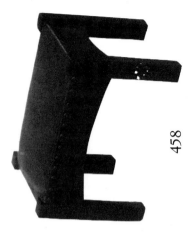

458

460

470

78   *Waste Basket, Plant Stand, Footrest*

No.			No.		
264	Rocker	$22.00	1916	Chair	$14.00
265	Chair	22.00	1919	Rocker	16.00
368	Rocker	12.50	475	Rocker	27.00
370	Chair	12.50	485	Chair	8.00
402	Settee	26.00	1340	Chair	8.00
380	Rocker	8.00	913	Chair	6.00
381	Chair	8.00	913½	Chair	7.00
384	Rocker	17.00	186	Morris Chair	25.00
386	Rocker	16.00	284	Morris Chair	22.00
422	Rocker	13.50	471	Morris Chair	23.00
424	Rocker	15.00	272	Davenport	50.00
425	Chair	15.00	274	Davenport	52.00
428	Rocker	27.00	230	Davenport	52.00
429	Chair	27.00	600	Davenport	75.00
430	Rocker	10.50	295	Couch	50.00
431	Chair	10.50	206	Foot Stool	3.25
433	Settee	22.00	436	Foot Stool	6.00
456	Rocker	12.50	397	Foot Stool	7.00
457	Chair	12.50	452	Magazine Rack	10.00
466	Rocker	14.00	558	Taborette	3.50
467	Chair	14.00	664	Telephone Stand	7.50
468	Settee	29.00	601	Desk	15.00
482	Rocker	10.50	661	Table	20.00
483	Chair	10.50	524	Table	44.00
484	Settee	22.00	392	Table	23.50
492	Rocker	14.00	374	Table	23.50
493	Chair	14.00	480	Table	28.00
494	Settee	29.00	388	Table	15.00
518	Rocker	15.50	276	Table, 30"	10.00
519	Chair	15.50	276	Table, 36"	12.50
520	Settee	32.00	276	Table, 42"	17.00
518	Rocker, Upholstered back	18.00	276	Table, 48"	25.00
519	Chair, Upholstered back	18.00	599	Table, 32x48	26.25
520	Settee, Upholstered back	37.00	599	Table, 32x54	29.00
640	Rocker	6.00	599	Table, 32x60	31.50
641	Chair	6.00	599	Table, 32x72	35.00
660	Chair	7.50	599	Table, 42x84	67.50
1917	Rocker	14.00			

All Upholstered Pieces are made in Genuine Leather
Mahogany and Walnut Finishes on   irch 5 percent extra
Terms: 2 percent 30, net 60, F. O. B. Camden

CHAIR (No. 425)
Rocker 424 to Match
Size, 47½ in. High, 23¾ in. Wide

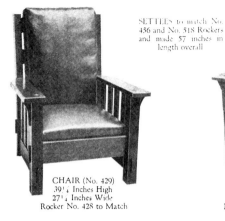

SETTEES to match No.
456 and No. 518 Rockers
and made 57 inches in
length overall

CHAIR (No. 429)
39¼ Inches High
27¼ Inches Wide
Rocker No. 428 to Match

CHAIR (No. 457)
39¼ Inches High
23½ Inches Wide
No. 456 Rocker to Match

YOUNG CHAIRS are made to the following Specifications: White Quartered Oak;
Genuine Spanish Leather; Automobile Spring
Cushion; all joints
mortised and
pinned

CHAIR (No. 519)
No. 518 Rocker to Match
Size, 39¼ in. High, 24¾ in. Wide

No. 392 TABLE
Size, 28x48 Inches
No. 524 with 3 Drawers, 32x60 Inches

No. 272 DAVENPORT. 60 Spring Auto Seat Cushion
Size, 34½ Inches High, 81 Inches Wide

Established 1873   J. M. Young's Sons   CAMDEN, N. Y.
CHAIR MANUFACTURERS

YOUNG
CHAIRS

❧

Your Office is as Important
As Your Home

▾

Equip It with Serviceable
Comfortable, Dependable
Furniture

❧

YOUNG'S IS ALL OF THESE

YOUNG—Dependable Furniture Since 1873

INCLUDE Chairs, Rockers, Settees, Davenports, Morris Chairs and Tables. Their careful construction is indicated by the careful mortising and pinning of all joints. Wooden pins being used on the front joints. The front posts on all pieces are mortised through the arms and pinned.   All chair cushions having sixteen springs.   We will be very glad to quote prices on your requirements.

No. 641
Size, 39¼ Inches High
16½ Inches Wide

No. 647
70 in. High

No. 643
Size, 39¼ Inches High, 47¼ Inches Wide

No. 645
39¼ Inches High, 23¼ Inches Wide
Rocker to Match

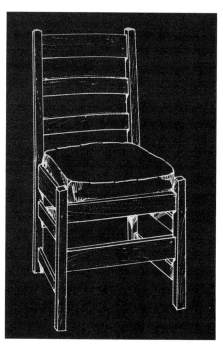

no. 800 Cushion Chair (1940)

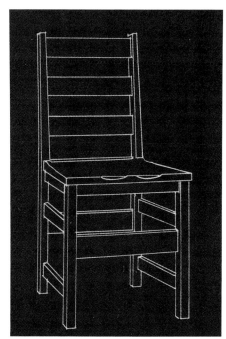

no. 954 Flag-Seat Chair (1939)

no. 470 Reclining Chair (1938)

no. 230 Settle (1934)

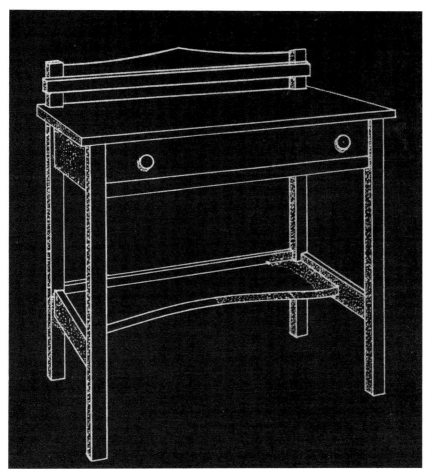

no. 601 Writing Desk (1935)

A Table of J. M. Young's Mission Pieces

This table lists all J. M. Young style numbers that fall within the mission period and within the range of other known mission style numbers. Where information is available, the table includes the name of the object, its first and last production dates, an estimate of the number of pieces sold, and its dimensions. The number in square brackets, in the second column, refers to the page in the Retail Plates section of this book showing a photograph or drawing of that object. A page number in parentheses refers to the V.A. blueprints or Young brochure.

Style numbers: Readers should be aware that the same style number may refer to different objects. This duplication originated in the Young journals and ledgers.

Dates and dimensions: Based on available documentation, both the dates and dimensions are reasonably accurate. However, significant gaps in the source materials affect sales totals and production dates for pieces made after 1930. The reader should keep this in mind when estimating the rarity of a given piece. A reminder, too, that dimensions of a piece may change without a corresponding change of style number.

Measurements: In the Dimensions column, widths are measured from the outside edges of the front posts—which seems to be the common method of measuring during the period. In some cases, width sizes for armchairs may refer to the distance between the outsides of the arms. Similar measurements occur in the Stickley catalogs.

Settles and Davenports: In the Victorian spirit, Young's journals occasionally refer to the "Davenport" as a synonym for "settle." For clarity's sake, the table uses "settle" throughout for this kind of furniture.

Style	Page	Object	PRODUCTION DATES First	Last	Sold	Dimensions
2	[75]	Single-door bookcase	——	——	——	H: 55" W: 30" D: 12"
3	[76]	Double-door bookcase	——	——	——	H: 55" W: 36" D: 12"
5		Triple-door bookcase	——	——	——	
45		Stickley bookstand	1928	——	——	
89		Costumer	1927	1929	7	
103	[69]	Dresser with triple mirror	*ca.*1930	*ca.*1936	——	W: 48" D: 22"
150	[7]	Rocker	1904	1917	703	H: 35¾" W: 22½"
150½		Rocker	1905	1912	74	
152	[7]	Armchair	1904	1919	492	H: 38¾" W: 22½"
——		Settee to match no. 152	1904	1915	5	

Style	Page	Object	PRODUCTION DATES First	Last	Sold	Dimensions
152½		Chair	1905	1912	28	
154	[8]	Rocker	1940	1940	9	
155	[8]	Armchair	1938	1938	6	H: 38″ W: 26″
158		Rocker	1904	1913	565	
158½	[9]	Rocker	1905	1916	470	H: 35″ W: 23½″
158½		Settee	1910	1914	8	
160		Chair	1904	1914	419	
160½	[9]	Armchair	1905	1915	228	H: 38¾″ W: 22½″
162		?	1904	1905	8	
162½		?	1904	1904	6	
164		Settee?	1904	1905	7	
166		?	1904	1906	28	
168		?	1904	1907	18	
170		Table	1904	1905	10	
172		?	1904	1906	17	
174		Chair/Rocker?	1904	1910	37	
176		Chair/Rocker?	1904	1914	127	
178		?	1905	1905	1	
180	[55]	Round/square table	1904	1920	391	24″ × 24″/ 28″ × 28″
182	[57]	Trestle table	1904	1914/1920	144	
182½		Table	1912	1912	4	
184	[47]	Settee	1904	1917	349	H: 38¾″ W: 45½″
184½		Settee	1907	1917	68	
186	[24]	Morris chair	1904	1940s	2,133	H: 38″ W: 27½″
186a		Morris chair	1918	——	——	
186½		Morris chair rocker	——	——	——	
188	[1]	Rocker	1904	1918	343	
188½		Rocker	1909	1909	2	
189	[1]	Chair	1905	1923	725	
——		Armchair to match no. 189	1912	1914	4	
189½		Chair	1907	1912	17	
190		?	1904	1905/1915	50	
192		?	1904	1906/1916	20	
194		?	1905	1905	2	
198		Chair	1905	1910	157	
200		Rocker	1905	1918	489	
200½		Rocker	1911	1911	1	
202		Chair	1905	1915	335	
204	[77]	Umbrella stand	1905	1924	482	
204		Chair	1929	1929	12	
206	[71]	Footrest [footstool]	1905	early 30s	4,568	H: 17″ W: 13″ D: 18″

| Style | Page | Object | PRODUCTION DATES | | Sold | Dimensions |
			First	Last		
208	[61]	Table	1905	1922	300	D: 12″ × L: 36″/ 28″ × 48″/ 60″ × 32″/ 36″ × 72″
210	[58]	Table	1905	1926	386	D: 24″ × L: 36″
212		Table	1905	1907	7	
214		?	1906	1910	117	
216		?	1906	1911	61	
218		Round table	1906	1906	5	Diam: 36″/42″/48″
220		?	1906	1906	5	
223		Settee with 2 or 4 pillows	1908	1908	3	
224		Rocker	1906	1913	245	
224½		Rocker	1908	1911	7	
226		Chair	1906	1913	157	
226½		Chair	1908	1912	5	
228	[31]	Rocker	1906	1918	463	
228½		Rocker	1911	1911	2	
230	[31]	Armchair	1906	1918	278	
230	[48(84)]	Settle	1910	1940	138	H: 29½″ W: 78½″
230½		Chair	1911	1911	2	
232		?	1907	1910	13	
234		?	1906	1916	204	
236		?	1906	1906	5	
238		?	1906	1906	3	
240	[72]	Magazine rack	1906	1920	301	
242	[59]	Desk	1907	1918/1921	381	28″ × 36″
242		Plant stand	1906	1917	11	
242½		Desk	1911	1911	3	
244		Table	1907	1907	2	
246		Settee	1907	1908	3	
248		?	1907	1907	53	
250		Chair	1907	1918	321	
252		Chair	1907	1908	16	
254		Chair	1908	1908	6	
254½		Chair	1908	1908	4	
256		?	1907	1910	12	
256½		?	1908	1910	2	
260		Small chair	1908	1908	15	
260		?	1913	1913	1	
261		?	1911	1911	1	
262		Chair?	1910	1910	2	
262		Settee with 2 pillows	1908	1908	2	
262½		Chair?	1910	1910	1	
264	[25]	Rocker	1908	1939/1943	480	
265	[26]	Armchair	1911	1930s	290	H: 39¼″ W: 25″

Style	Page	Object	PRODUCTION DATES First	Last	Sold	Dimensions
266		Settee	1909	1912	13	W: 84"
268	[49]	Settle	1908	1919	102	L: 28"/72"/78"
270		Settee	1908	1910	5	
270		?	1913	1913	2	
272	[50,51 (80)]	Settle	1909	1942	701	H: 34" W: 78½"
272½		Settee	1929	1929	1	
274	[52]	Settle	1908	1929	446	H: 34" W: 78½"
276	[56]	Round table	1908	1941	241	Diam: 20"/36"/40"/ 42"/48"
278	[56]	Round table	1908–1919	1926–1927	109	Diam: 30"/36"/42"/54"
280		?	1908	1912	171	
281		Settee with 4 pillows	1908	1908	2	
282		?	1908	1910	102	
284	[27]	Morris chair	1908	1941	1,784	H: 38" W: 26"
284	[27]	Fixed-back morris chair	1916	1925	14	H: 38" W: 26"
284		Rocker	1911	1929	38	H: 35" W: 26"
284		Fixed-back rocker	1916	1925	14	H: 35" W: 26"
284½		?	1911	1915	55	
285		Fixed-back rocker	1911	1911	2	H: 35½" W: 26"
286		?	1908	1909	16	
286½		?	1908	1908	4	
288	[10]	Rocker	1908	1916	201	H: 35¾" W: 23½"
289	[10]	Armchair	1909	1916	102	H: 39½" W: 23½"
290	[60]	Table	1908	1919	90	
291		Couch	1908	1908	2	
292		?	1909	1915	54	
294		Settee?	1909	1911	48	
295	[54]	Daybed (couch)	1926	1943	671	H: 22½" L: 72½" W: 28"
300		Rocker	1909	1912	20	
301		Chair?	1912	1912	1	
302		Chair/Rocker?	1910	1910	2	
304		Plant stand	1909	1912	15	
306		Chair/Rocker?	1909	1909	1	
306		Plant stand	1910	1910	1	
308	[32]	Armchair	1909	1925	792	
308½		Armchair	1909	1909	1	
310	[32]	Rocker	1909	1925	1,215	
310½		Rocker	1909	1909	1	
312		Chair with 3-slat back	1909	1910	28	

Style	Page	Object	PRODUCTION DATES First	Last	Sold	Dimensions
313		?	1909	1909	6	
314		Chair	1909	1919	1,474	
——		Settee to match no. 314	1910	1910	1	
314½		Chair	1911	1911	1	
315		Chair	1909	1919	111	
316		Chair	1909	1916	175	
317		?	1909	1912	91	
318		?	1913	1916	3	
320		Footrest	1909	1912	52	
324		Settee	1909	1913	12	
326		Chair/Rocker?	1909	1913	8	
328		Chair/Rocker?	1909	1911	35	
330		Chair/Rocker?	1909	1916	22	
331		Settee	1910	1910	1	
332		Chair	1909	1912	75	
334	[32]	Settee	1910	1923	317	
336	[33]	Rocker	1910	1920	333	
338	[33]	Armchair	1910	1920	274	
——		Settee to match no. 338	1912	1912	1	
342	[55]	Taboret	1910	1917	70	
344		Chair/Rocker?	1910	1913	30	
344		Table	1913	1913	1	D: 28″ × L: 60″
346		Rocker?	1910	1911	21	
348		Chair?	1910	1910	5	
350		Settee?	1910	1911	10	
352	[28]	Morris chair	1910	1912	25	
354		?	1910	1912	10	
356		?	1910	1912	52	
358	[20]	Cane-back armchair	1910	1911	10	
359		?	1910	1911	4	
360		Chair	1910	1917	37	
360		Settee	1910	1910	1	
360½		Chair	1910	1910	1	
362		Chair	1910	1914	104	
363		?	1912	1912	6	
364	[11]	Rocker	1910	1916	92	
366	[11]	Armchair	1910	1913	39	
368		Rocker	1910	1946	1,866	
368		?	1912	1912	1	
368½	[12]	Rocker	1911	1919	704	
——		Settee to match nos. 368½ & 370½	1911	1911	2	
370		Chair	1910	1943	697	H: 38¼″ W: 23½″
370½	[12]	Armchair	1911	1919	493	H: 39¼″ W: 23½″

Style	Page	Object	PRODUCTION DATES First	Last	Sold	Dimensions
372	[33]	Settee	1910	1918	86	H: 38½″ W: 44″
374	[62]	Table	1910	1944	655	D: 28″ × L: 42″
376		Chair/Rocker?	1910	1911	5	
378	[34]	Rocker	1910	1915	76	
379	[34]	Armchair	1911	1915	69	
380	[2]	Rocker	1911	1939	539	H: 34″ W: 18″
380		Settee	1910	1911	3	
381	[2]	Chair	1909	1946	2,211	H: 37″–37½″ W: 18″–18½″
——		Armchair to match no. 381	1914	1928	7	
381½		Chair	1915	1929	48	
382	[71]	Footrest	1911	1927	358	
382½		Footrest	1912	1912	1	
384	[22]	High-back rocker	1911	1939	536	H: 42½″ W: 23¾″
384½		High-back rocker	1911	1912	10	H: 42½″ W: 23¾″
385		?	1911	1926	9	
386	[13]	Rocker	1911	1929	361	
386½	[13]	Rocker	1911	1917	17	
——		Chair to match no. 386½	1911	1911	3	
387		Chair	1912	1928	31	
388	[64]	Table	1911	1958	1,296	D: 24″ × L: 36″/ 22″ × 32″/ 26″ × 42″
389	[63]	Desk chair	1911	1922	171	
389½		Desk chair, higher back	1916	1917	12	
390	[63]	Desk	1911	1921	167	D: 24″ × L: 36″
391		Drumhead-seat chair	1911	1912	11	
392	[64]	Table	1911	1949	968	D: 28″ ×L: 48″/ 28″ × 60″/ 28″ × 54″/ 34″ × 72″
394		?	1911	1911	1	
396		Chair/Rocker?	1911	1911	2	
397	[71]	Footrest	1927	1930s	65	D: 15″ × L: 19″
397		Chair	1911	1911	2	
398		Settee?	1911	1911	2	
400		Chair/Rocker?	1911	1913	12	
402	[47]	Settee	1911	1929	164	H: 39½″ W: 54″, 72″
404	[54]	Daybed (couch)	1911	1926	102	
406		Telephone table	1911	1912	2	
407		Telephone stool	1911	1912	2	
408		Piano stool	1911	1913	6	

| Style | Page | Object | PRODUCTION DATES | | Sold | Dimensions |
			First	Last		
410		Bookrack	1911	1911	4	
410		Bookrack with door	1911	1911	1	
412	[21]	Rocker	1911	1912	14	
413		Chair?	1911	1911	1	
414		Rocker	1911	1912	5	
414		Settee to match no. 230	1911	1911	1	
415		Chair	1911	1912	8	
416	[31]	Settee	1912	1915	26	
418	[35]	Rocker	1912	1919	200	H: 36¼″ W: 23¼″
418½		Rocker	1912	1912	1	
419	[35]	Armchair	1912	1920	181	H: 39¼″ W: 23¼″
419½		Chair	1912	1912	2	
420	[35]	Settee	1912	1919	42	
421		?	1920	1920	1	
422	[21]	Rocker	1912	1928	1,941	
423		?	1912	1923	27	
424		Chair to match no. 492	1915	1915	2	
424	[14]	High-back rocker	1912	1939/1943	1,128	H: 44″ W: 27″ D: 20″
• 424ws	[14]	High-back rocker, wood seat	post-1930	1939	21	H: 44″ W: 27″ D: 20″
424½		Rocker with back pad	1916	1918	13	
425	[14(80)]	High-back armchair	1916	1928/1943	312	
426	[34]	Settee	1911	1914	12	
428	[29]	Fixed-back morris rocker	1912	1938	117	
429	[29(80)]	Fixed-back morris chair	1912	1941	189	H: 39″ W: 27½″
430	[36]	Rocker	1912	1946	3,372	
———		Settee to match no. 430	1919	1919	6	
430½		Chair with side panels	1913	1914	2	
431	[36]	Armchair	1912	1939	2,128	H: 39″ W: 23¾″
———		Side chair to match no. 431	1914	1917	4	
431½		Chair with side panels	1913	1920	3	H: 39″ W: 23¾″
432		Settee? to match nos. 431, 433	1912	1914	11	
433	[36]	Settee	1912	1938	328	H: 39½″ W: 47½″
433½		Settee to match nos. 430½, 431½	1913	1913	1	
434	[61]	Table	1912	1925	226	
435	[37]	Settee	1912	1914	23	

Style	Page	Object	PRODUCTION DATES First	Last	Sold	Dimensions
436	[37]	Rocker	1912	1921	164	
436	[71]	Footrest ["stretcher"]	1912	1928	407	H: 17″ W: 19″ D: 15″
437	[37]	Armchair	1912	1918	66	
438		Rocker	1912	1917	165	
438½		Rocker	1914	1914	1	
439		Chair	1912	1917	144	
439		Rocker	1908	1908	1	
440		Settee	1912	1916	46	W: 55″
———		Chair to match no. 440	1913	1913	1	
———		Rocker to match no. 440	1913	1913	1	
442		Settee?	1912	1914	2	
444		?	1912	1913	3	
445	[38]	Armchair	1913	1919	256	H: 39¼″ W: 23⅜″ D: 19¼″
———		Side chair to match no. 445	1913	1915	3	
446	[38]	Rocker	1912	1917	419	H: 39¼″ W: 23⅜″ D: 19⅛″
447		Rocker	1908	1908	1	
447	[38]	Settee	1913	1917	95	H: 42½″ W: 39¾″ D: 19¼″
448	[15]	Drumhead-seat rocker	1913	1914	22	
449	[15]	Drumhead-seat armchair	1913	1916	18	
449		Rocker	1908	1908	1	
452	[73]	Magazine rack	1913	1941	268	H: 43¾″ W: 21¾″ D: 13½″
454	[16]	Rocker	1913	1918	29	
455	[16]	Armchair	1913	1917	21	
———		Settle to match nos. 454, 455	1914	1914	1	
456	[17]	"Stickley" rocker	1913	*ca.* 1930	1,137	H: 34½″ W: 23½″
———		Side chair to match no. 456	1917	1917	1	
457	[17(80)]	"Stickley Chair" [armchair]	1913	1942	670	H: 39″ W: 23½″
———		Side chair to match no. 457	1916	1917	———	
———		Settee to match nos. 456, 457	1917	1917	2	

| Style | Page | Object | PRODUCTION DATES | | Sold | Dimensions |
			First	Last		
457½		Chair	1920	1929	13	
458	[78]	Footrest	1913	1927	47	
458		Wood-seat settee	1928	1928	1	H: 39″ W: 55″
459		Settee	1913	1914	2	
460	[78]	Plant stand	1913	1915	14	
462		Book/magazine rack	1913	1915	5	H: 31″ W: 12½″
464		Settle	1913	1917	22	W: 72″
466	[39]	Rocker	1913	1959	1,113	
467	[39]	Armchair	1913	1959	2,823	H: 39″ W: 23¼″
468	[39]	Settee to match no. 466	1913	1930	113	H: 39½″ W: 47½″
——		Chair to match no. 468½ [?]	1916	1916	1	
470	[78]	Waste basket	1913	1917	20	
470	[(83)]	Reclining chair	——	——	——	
471	[30]	Morris chair	1925	1939	21	H: 38″ W: 28″
472		Round table	1913	1917	62	H: 28″ Diam: 24″
474		Square table	1913	1916	16	H: 28″ W: 22″ D: 22″
475	[30]	Stickley-pattern morris rocker	1925	1930s	48	H: 36″ W: 26″
476		Morris chair	1913	1930s	619	
476		Morris chair with rockers	1913	1913	5	
476½		Morris chair	1914	1914	3	
478		Desk	1913	1922	91	D: 20¼″ × L: 32″
480	[65]	Table	1913	1949	1,046	D: 28″ × L: 48″
480		Chair?	1911	1911	5	
481		?	1911	1911	4	
482	[40]	Rocker	1913	1946	4,687	
483	[40]	Armchair	1913	1944	3,169	H: 39″ W: 23¼″
——		Side chair to match no. 483	1915	1916	7	
483½		Chair	1920	1920	1	
484	[40]	Settee	1913	1939	647	H: 39½″ W: 47½″ or 60″ or 72″
485	[5]	Chair	1927	1946	73	
485		Hall tree	1914	1914	1	
486		Footrest	1914	1916	5	
486		Morris chair	1914	1919	92	
487		Chair with panels	1914	1914	1	
488		Cane-back rocker	1914	1916	68	
489	[41]	Group: armchair, settee, rocker	1914	1916	26	
490		?	1915	1915	1	

Style	Page	Object	PRODUCTION DATES		Sold	Dimensions
			First	Last		
492	[42]	Rocker	1914	ca.1930	1,087	
493	[42]	Armchair	1914	ca.1939	870	H: 39″ W: 24½″
493½		Chair	1916	1927	23	H: 39¼″ W: 24½″
494	[42]	Settee	1914	1940	242	H: 39″ W: 55″
494½		Settee with upholstered back	1927	1927	1	H: 39″
495		Table	1914	1917	38	
496		Small rocker	1914	1918	23	
497		Small chair	1914	1917	54	
498		?	1915	1915	1	
499		?	1915	1916	121	
———		Armchair to match no. 499	1915	1915	1	
500 Special	[6]	Chair	ca.1938	———	———	
500	[43]	Rocker	1915	1926	909	H: 36½″ W: 23½″
501	[43]	Armchair	1915	1926	678	H: 39½″ W: 23½″
502	[43]	Settee	1915	1924	299	
504		Table	1915	1922	198	
505		Checkerboard table	1926	1927	25	D: 30″ × L: 48″
506		Rocker	1915	1917	300	
507		Chair	1915	1920	434	
507½		Chair	1915	1915	1	
508		Settee	1915	1917	76	
509		Table	1915	1916	59	
510		Chair/Rocker?	1915	1915	4	
511		Table	1915	1927	4	
514		Stickley table	1917	1926	15	
515		Chair/Rocker?	1915	1939	9	
518	[44]	Rocker	1915	1946	1,290	H: 36″ W: 24½″
518½		Rocker	1917	1929	5	
519	[44(80)]	Armchair	1915	1949	2,796	H: 39″ W: 24½″
519½		Chair	1917	1929	90	
520	[44]	Settee	1915	1942	281	H: 39″ W: 55″
520½		Settee	1929	1929	1	
522		Table	1908	1921	2	
523		Rocker	1916	1921	5	
524	[66]	Table	1926	1939	52	D: 32″ × L: 60″/ 32″ × 72″
527		?	1917	1917	1	
530		?	1915	1916	3	
531		Rocker	1915	1927	13	
537		Table	1908	1916	4	
538		Rocker?	1915	1918	27	
539		Chair?	1915	1918	21	

| Style | Page | Object | PRODUCTION DATES | | Sold | Dimensions |
			First	Last		
540		Settee?	1916	1917	8	
542		Rocker	1915	1916	10	
543		Chair	1915	1917	11	
544		Table	1908	1916	4	D: 48″ × L: 48″
544		Settee	1916	1916	1	
546		?	1915	1916	3	
548		Footrest	1915	1920	86	
550		Settee?	1916	1916	4	
552		Table	1929	1929	5	
555		Table with caning	1916	1917	32	D: 28″ × L: 48″
558	[55]	Taboret	1929	1941	10	H: 17″ or 20″ W: 15″ or 18″
562		Small rocker	1916	1919	2	
564		Small chair?	1916	1919	8	
564		Table	1908	1908	1	
566	[45]	Rocker	1916	1925	273	
567	[45]	Armchair	1916	1925	135	
568	[45]	Settee	1916	1927	42	
570		Settee with upholstered arms	1916	1916	1	
572	[22]	High-back rocker	1916	1927	326	
572		Checkerboard table	1927	1929	6	
582	[46]	Rocker	1916	1927	292	
583	[46]	Armchair	1916	1926	133	
584	[46]	Settee	1916	1926	92	
587		Chair	1920	1926	30	
588		Settee	1920	1921	13	
590	[23]	Rocker	1918	1927	356	
591		Chair?	1918	1924	83	H: 39¼″ W: 23¼″
592		?	1920	1920	2	
599	[57]	Trestle table	1927	1940	99	D: 32″ × L: 48″/ 32″ ×54″/ 32″ ×60″/ 32″ ×72″/ 42″ × 84″
600	[53]	Settle	1922	1941	34	H: 34″ W: 78½″
600		Desk	1927	1927	1	D: 32″ × L: 60″
600		?	1922	1922	1	
601	[67(85)]	Desk	1926	1945	152	H: 34¾″ L: 34″ W: 20″
602		Desk	1926	1927	30	D: 22″ × L: 40″
626		Chair?	1923	1928	344	
627	[6]	Chair with saddle seat	1924	1939	1,058	H: 35¾″ W: 16½″
——		Rocker to match no. 627	1927	1927	10	

Style	Page	Object	PRODUCTION DATES First	Last	Sold	Dimensions
628	[23]	Rocker	1920s	1920s	——	
629		Chair to match no. 628	1920s	1920s	——	
631		Dresser/bureau	1929	1929	3	
633		Chiffonnier	1929	1929	13	
640	[3]	Rocker	1925	1938	105	
640		Taboret	1925	1927	45	
641	[3(81)]	Chair	1925	1959	5,429	H: 35¾" W: 16½"
641		Bookcase	1927	1929	9	
643	[(81)]	Settee	1925	1939	14	H: 39" W: 47¼"
644		Chair/Rocker?	1923	1939	9	
645	[(81)]	Armchair	1925	1940	48	H: 39" W: 23¼"
645		Stickley bookcase	1928	1928	2	
647		Bookcase	1927	——	——	H: 52" W: 72"
647	[(81)]	Hall tree/costumer	1925	1929	——	H: 70"
660	[19]	Chair with tablet arm	1925	1943	1,949	H: 35½" W: 19¼"
661	[68]	Table with drawer	1926	1946	421	D: 18" × L: 30"/ 30" ×48"/ 32" ×48"/ 32" ×54"/ 32" × 60"
663	[19]	Billiard chair	1908	1930s	128	H: 42" W: 23"
664	[70]	Telephone stand and stool	1927	1929	54	
667		Stool	1930	1930	6	
670		?	1923	1923	6	
680		Chair/Rocker?	1929	1929	1	
692½		?	1908	1908	6	
700		Settle	1938	1958	532	
700½		Settle	1938	1959	835	
706		Sideboard	1927	1928	13	D: 20" × L: 48"
707		Sideboard	1929	1929	3	
751		Serving table	1927	1929	33	D: 16" × L: 38"
752		Side table	1927	1927	3	
786		?	1909	1909	1	
787		?	1909	1909	1	
800	[(82)]	Chair	1926	1947	190	H: 36¼"
801		Rocker	1929	1929	9	
804		?	1927	1927	2	
805		?	1927	1929	19	
810		Stickley pattern?	1925	1925	4	
811		Stickley pattern?	1925	1925	8	
820		Stickley-pattern chair	1928	1928	8	
830		Morris chair	1929	1929	5	
835		Chair	1916	1916	1	

Style	Page	Object	PRODUCTION DATES First	Last	Sold	Dimensions
836		Settee	1927	1927	1	
836		Settle	1916	1916	1	
837		Chair	1927	1927	4	
844		?	1908	1908	1	
847		?	1927	1927	2	
913	[4]	Chair, wood seat	1926	1945	520	H: 38" W: 16½" D: 16"
913½	[4]	Chair, covered seat	1941	1944	4	H: 38" W: 17"
944		Chair	1926	1927	17	
946		Chair	1927	1930	3	
946½		Chair	1927	1929	25	
950		?	1927	1928	52	
953		Chair	1908	1908	84	
953½		Chair?	1908	1908	53	
954	[(82)]	Flag-seat chair	——	——	——	
957	[19]	Rocker	——	——	——	H: 34½" W: 23"
960		Chair with tablet arm	1926	1928	125	
1340	[5]	Chair	1926	1940	311	H: 35" W: 16¾" D: 15¾"
——		Armchair to match no. 1340	1927	1927	1	
1344		Chair	1926	1927	20	
1354		Chair	1927	1929	70	
1914		Table	1926	1929	6	
1916	[18]	Armchair	1927	1944	160	H: 39" W: 23½" D: 19½"
1917	[18]	Rocker	1927	1940	282	H: 35½" W: 23½"
1917½		Rocker	1927	1929	29	
1918		Stickley-pattern morris chair	1926	1929	51	
1919	[18]	High-back rocker	1927	1939	199	H: 39" W: 23½"
1920		Settee?	1927	1927	1	
1922		Settee	1927	1929	14	